TRIUMPH THROUGH PAIN

*How to Maximize
Your Full Potential
During Dark Times*

Basiliso Moreno, LMSW

Triumph Through Pain: How to Maximize Your Full Potential During Dark Times.

DISCLAIMER

The advice contained in this material might not be suitable for everyone. The author designed the information to present his opinion about the subject matter. The reader must carefully investigate all aspects of any business decision before committing him or herself. The author obtained the information contained herein from sources he believes to be reliable and from his own personal experience, but he neither implies nor intends any guarantee of accuracy. The author is not in the business of giving legal, accounting, or any other type of professional advice. Should the reader need such advice, he or she must seek services from a competent professional. The author particularly disclaims any liability, loss, or risk taken by individuals who directly or indirectly act on the information contained herein. The author believes the advice presented here is sound, but readers cannot hold him responsible for either the actions they take or the risk taken by individuals who directly or indirectly act on the information contained herein.

Published by Bas City Entertainment LLC

Printed in the United States
Cover Design by @Sharon Avnon

TABLE OF CONTENTS

ACKNOWLEDGEMENTS

First and foremost, thank you God for all of your blessings. Without you, there's no me. To my coach, Ash Cash, thank you for your knowledge and helping me reach this goal of being a published author. To Rashad Bilal and Troy Millings of the *Earn Your Leisure* podcast, thank you for your platform. I have learned so much since the pandemic has started. I have tried to put things into practice and to execute and achieve my goals.

To my colleagues and coaches, Rosalyn Ortega-Elie (@Urban-Teach_) and Michelle McAllister (@LandlordinStilettos), thank you ladies for all of your help and knowledge. I have learned a lot from you both. Let's continue to get that money.

Obviously, thank you to my fiancé Jenisse. Thank you for supporting me through all of my crazy ideas. Thank you for your understanding, your patience, and for always being there by my side. Te Amo.

DEDICATION

This book is dedicated to the over 900,000 people and counting who have lost their lives due to Covid-19. To those who lost loved ones, I offer my sincere condolences for your loss.

This book is dedicated to the 30 former clients who lost their lives due to Covid-19 from the non-profit where I worked when the pandemic started. May all of you continue to rest in peace. It was an honor serving you in one way or another.

Shout out to all the social workers and mental health professionals who have worked tirelessly to provide services to those in need and who have experienced various trauma as a result.

This book is also dedicated to my son Elijah and my daughter Sophia. This book is about leaving a legacy. You can always go back, read these words from the book, and say to yourselves, "Wow, Daddy wrote a book, how cool!" (Well, you'd better say that, lol). I love you both forever and always. Everything I do, I do it for you.

INTRODUCTION

This book has been written in chronological order from April 2020 to June 2021, during the worst period of my professional life when I experienced almost daily vicarious trauma as a result of my clients at my job passing away from Covid-19. My home life began to mirror my work life, having to call 911 on my mother who began choking from simply drinking some Gatorade.

Throughout the months, I saw police kill unarmed African-Americans, gyms closing down, the President acting a fool on a daily basis, and, of course, a global pandemic unfold.

Out of the blue, poetry became an outlet to relieve the build-up of all this stress, anxiety, and trauma. Then, I found the self-awareness to still want to achieve my goals, to learn new things, and to better myself and my family.

If my story inspires just one person, I'll be more than satisfied. To quote dancehall artist Baby Cham, "This is a survival story."

CHAPTER 1

BEING HOPEFUL THROUGH SURVIVAL

Through hurt and pain, dealing with my own sorrow
Can't believe what is going on within my own borough
Deep hurt, deep pain, but getting through each day
Still can't believe my mom got taken away
My hero, my Queen, How I love you so
Why bad cops keep killing our bros??

Damn pandemic got us calling for paramedics
Underlying conditions, almost equals your ultimate demise
Those who survive, asking how can we thrive??
Lord, I'm just trying to survive.

I'm just trying to stack bread,
Buying bread, trying to eat
Thankful I can still get to work using my feet

When will it end? When will it stop?
Lord knows, but know I'm in God's hands
God blessed me to give back to my peeps, to my peers, my kids

Can't you see, despite my loss, I still have a lot to see
Weddings, meeting friends babies

Let the world be cleaned,
No more orange stench dividing our nation.
Come on now pay attention!
We are writing history as we speak.

Take it one day at a time.

Damn you Pandemic!!

CHAPTER 2

TEXT OR EMAIL

Imagine living in a world where the only way to ID
Your dead relative was via Text or Email

That was my reality, mom passed
When the coroner called me to ID the body
My options were Text or email

Thanks Covid

Fucking text or email, the worst email I've ever received
Can't believe my eyes,
My eyes not deceiving me

I just lost a piece of me
Moments away from passing out
Cold water saving me
Thanks again son for the water
As life was fading from me

Damn email, shit is etched in me
Tattooed in my mind, for my eternity

Damn email.

CHAPTER 3

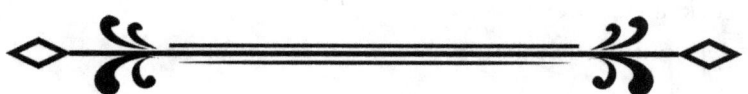

DEAR MOMMA

Hola momma
Just wanted to say I miss you.
I miss your cooking.
I miss your laugh.
I miss watching wrestling with you.
I miss you eating my Rona snacks.
I miss correcting you on the pronunciation of Zumba.
I miss you asking me "Esiste el baile?" (talking about me teaching Zumba)
I miss you cursing out Trump (Ha Ha).
I miss you having girl talk with Titi Gloria.
The kids miss you.
Dad misses you.
I miss you.
I thank you.
Dear Momma, I love you.

CHAPTER 4

MY MVP OF QUARANTINE

Shout out to my MVP of quarantine
That fly girl that be representing Queens
Jenisse is her name
Smart girl, dope girl, always loving me
Thank you for all that you do
Just wanted to let you know
How much I love you so
Look forward to spending the rest of my life with you
My love for you is so so true.
Thank you again for all that you do
Mi Amor te amo
My MVP!

CHAPTER 5

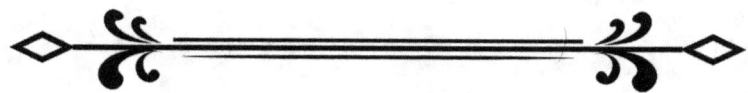

I GOT THE KEYS

I got all the keys,
House keys,
Car keys,
Keys to my lady's heart
Just trying to do my part
Living life through Christ
Beyond blessed through all of his glory
I'm just here telling you my story
Through hurt and pain
Now celebrating my gains
Now get this knowledge to fill up my brain.
Learning about stocks, bonds and 401K's
Celebrating new home ownership for all of my days

CHAPTER 6

THE UNKNOWN

New job
New house
New rules
Covid running through
In the sky, oh my, fearing my potential demise
New state
Still wishing to get baked
Like the movie half baked
New business
Ready to say future Mrs.
Moreno that is
Number 2
My heart through and through
The known is here
But there's nothing to fear
Cause God has got me in the right gear.

CHAPTER 7

PANDEMIC BLUES

In a time full of masks, gloves and zoom calls,
UNMUTE YOURSELF!
While trying to live my best self
Worrying about one's health
At the same time learning to build wealth
Learning remotely, working remotely
The new norm is here
Just here, trying not to live in fear
Oh dear
What's going on here??
Can't go outside without your gear
Masks, gloves and face shields
Moved out the Bronx, now seeing nothing but fields
Thinking about my work trauma, giving me the chills
Gotta push through to pay these bills
Trying to take care of self
I know the deal
This whole situation got me all in my feels
In time we shall all heal.

CHAPTER 8

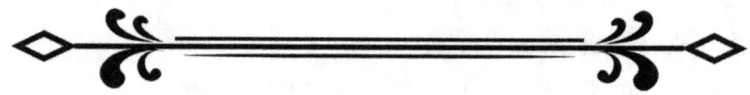

THE COME UP

We went from surviving and maintaining
To surviving and thriving
Trying to build a legacy
Building wealth no longer a fallacy,
Using my last name
It's time for us black and brown folks to be doing the same,
Generational wealth,
Health is wealth
Owning and growing,
Growing and owning stock portfolios, homes and businesses
Using all of this knowledge
So our kids can pay for college
Let's acknowledge
The time is now!
Shoot your shot
Why not?
Time for us black and brown to come up.

CHAPTER 9

BLESSED

Being alive is to be blessed
Waking up each morning, is to be blessed.
Blessed with two amazing kids.
Blessed with an amazing woman, full of kisses
Setting goals, completing goals, setting new ones
Having my girl beside me, when 2 become 1
Got a major goal to it,
The job is not done
Even in cloudy days
My new guardian angel provides the sun
Trying to leave a legacy for my handsome son
My beautiful daughter too
Blessed with you two
Daddy loves you two
Blessed to still have my dad
Hey God,
I thank you
Caused I'm truly blessed.

CHAPTER 10

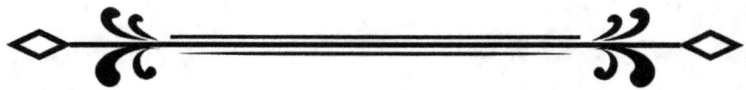

DEAR DAD

Dear Dad, I just want to say thank you
I love you
Learning from you has been the best gift you can give me
Learning from your mistakes
Relationships, Money, Parenting
Not saying this to play you
You've given me a playbook
Unconsciously to use for your grandkids
My kids,
For that all I can say is, thank you.

ABOUT THE AUTHOR

Basiliso (Bas) Moreno, is a Licensed Masters Level Social Worker in the state of Delaware. He also is a Certified School Social Worker in the state of Delaware. Bas graduated with his Masters in Social Work in 2010 from Fordham University School of Social Work in New York, NY. Bas received his Bachelors of Arts degree from Manhattan College where he majored in Communications and minored in Education.

Bas is a native of the Bronx, NY and is a father of two children Elijah and Sophia. Bas and family moved to Delaware in 2020.

Bas is also the founder of Bas City Entertainment LLC, established in 2020. Bas City Enterntainment, LLC focuses on providing his fellow social workers holistic online self-care with poetry and virtual Zumba classes.

Prior to the pandemic, Bas had been providing in person Zumba classes at a local gym in is native hometown of the Bronx, NY. He has been a licensed Zumba instructor since December 2018.

Basiliso is also the host of The Social Work Rants Podcast sharing his expertise about his world in Social Work.

Bas can be contacted via email at Bascityentertainmentllc@gmail.com

You can follow Bas on Instagram at @Bascityentertainmentllc; Tic Tok @Bascityentertainmentllc; and Facebook BasCity Entertainment LLC

His website is Basmoreno.com

www.ingramcontent.com/pod-product-compliance
Lightning Source LLC
Chambersburg PA
CBHW070454130626
46553CB00006B/2409